# Intimate Reflections

*poems by*

# Marie G. Fochios

*Finishing Line Press*
Georgetown, Kentucky

# Intimate Reflections

## ACKNOWLEDGMENTS

I wish to express my special gratitude to my family, the unwavering pillars
of my life. My daughter, Karen, has been instrumental in this creative
process, offering her extraordinary skills in proofreading and editing. My
deep appreciation goes to my daughter-in-law, Gretl, whose evocative cover
captures the essence of my book. To my husband, Steve, I owe boundless
thanks for his unending support and love. His steadfast belief in my abilities
and the countless hours he spent discussing my poetry were a constant source
of inspiration and motivation.

I am grateful to the following publications in which several of my poems first
appeared:
- *Echo* (Hunter College's Literary Magazine), 1944: "Variations on an Ode of
  Horace."
- *The New Verse News*, 2018: "Paradise Theater, 1936."
- *Passager*, 2021 poetry contest issue: "Memoir."

Publisher: Leah Huete de Maines
Editor: Christen Kincaid
Cover Art and Design: Gretl Bauer
Author Photo: David Fischer

Order online: www.finishinglinepress.com
also available on amazon.com

Author inquiries and mail orders:
Finishing Line Press
PO Box 1626
Georgetown, Kentucky 40324
USA

# Contents

Contents

*Dedicated to my muse, Sarah Stern*

## Memoir

The family asks me again and again. *Mom, why don't you write your memoir?* I give them many excuses. *Later, I don't have time right now.* They keep pestering me. *Mom, you have lots of time.* I smile and move away. *Perhaps some day soon*–but I know that day will never come. The past belongs to me alone.

labyrinthian
darkness and terror and rage
why would I return

**Paradise Theater, 1936**

Movie house where splicing comes unglued
and that malignant image
repeats itself again and again and again
indecent as a pistol shot penetrating,
entering a random target.

Fumbling, he grabs the child's hand
pressing down.
Only the darkness and the voices and the shadows
conceal the agony,
the hardening into a freeze frame.
Encrypted for life.
Until...
*#MeToo*

## Dad

It's not my fault I was born a girl.
That was your luck of the draw.
I tied back my hair, outraced
the kids on the block, jumped over hydrants,
shot marbles along the curb, but
you were immune to me.

**

It's 1940, Yankee Stadium. I cut class to find out what this game's all about. Why my dad glues his ear to the radio, never misses a broadcast. I buy a score card. No idea who the players are except for Joe DiMaggio. Even I know that name! Bottom of the ninth, a young rookie named Rizzuto pops a foul ball into the upper stands. The guy near me yells, "Hey, kid, know how lucky you are? Hurry, run to the back gate, where the players come out. Get them to sign your ball." I race to the exit. As the players push past the crowd, I hold up the ball and each one scrawls his name on it-except for DiMaggio who just shoves me aside. I run home and toss the ball to my dad.

**

*Can't believe that kid caught a ball.*
*Been going to games since 1911.*
*Never happened to me.*
*And that DiMaggio, not signing it.*
*Think he's better than my kid?*
*Wait till I tell the guys at work about her.*
*She's OK.*

**

But what if I hadn't caught the ball.

## Lament for Billy

*WW II*

I'm furious with you.
How could you abandon me?

Always together.
Sharing our poems.
You, a young Keats.
Me, Fanny Browne.

Dark clouds circled.
Uncle Sam pointed his finger and said,
I want you!
And off you went.

England, France, Germany.
Your poems kept coming.
Until silenced by all you saw.
That silence sent you home.

There you sat at your desk.
Stared at the blank paper.
Put down your pen.
Put the gun in your mouth.
Put the bullet in your head.

## The Queen Bee

Trapped in the dark interior of her cell,
she folds and unfolds her wings.
Flight memory stirs within her.

Fragments emerge
    silky milkweed
    lush fields of clover
    upright stigma of laurel blossoms
    impatient bees
circling, circling, circling.

Her body, desire.
She struggles out of her waxen cell,
grooms herself
with her long-forgotten essence,
throws on her black and gold robes.

Springing into the sky.
She is the sorceress, Medea
spewing her magic potion.
Earthward.

Her pursuers swarm upward.
Frenzied Maenads,
they dance madly around her
licking and squeezing
her hairy body.
She has not lost her scent.

## Dark Towers

ε έ. πικράν ες αρχαν βαίνεις

Ah, for the bitter story
that you still seek to know.
　　*Helen*, Euripides

Stumbling up the mountainside
the Greek sun unhinges my joints.
Not a tree relieves that skull-like landscape.
Lizards dart over the hot earth.
The village ahead with its stone towers
pierces the sky.

Across the square, old men
leaning on their canes
wave me over.

　　　　Are you Greek? So tell us. You're an attractive woman.
　　　　What do you think? Did Paris force Helen to go with him?
　　　　Or did she seduce him with her beauty?

*They stir the Helen in me. After all these centuries they're still talking?*
*Does anyone want to hear? Do you want to hear my bitter story? Me, the*
*daughter of Zeus and Leda? Theseus groped me when I was twelve, tore*
*away my virginity, abandoned me, found by my brothers who brought*
*me back to Sparta. Go, ask Menelaus why he married me. He damn well*
*knew about my powerful lineage. And that brother of his Agamemnon;*
*power hungry, the two of them. Then along came Paris, said he loved*
*me; words I always wanted to hear. Then I left my home, my family,*
*my children and ran off with him, little knowing he had won me in a*
*contest. In Troy, everyone hated me, women spit on me. The war ended*
*and Menelaus dragged me by my hair back to the Greek ships.*

The old men circle me.
"Well, what do you say?"

I want to speak,
but who will listen?

Only the myth endures.

## Lockerbie

*In Memoriam*
*Alexia*
*1968-1988*

This is what I saw
that December morning.

Bare trees.
People huddled around a grave.

A father, kneeling,
tracing her name in the snow.

Distant. Alone.
Still trapped in his private labyrinth.

He stumbles over mounds of scorched clothing,
crumbled baggage, shards of metal.

Gasping for air,
he can't look into the black plastic bag.

Daedalus knows.
It doesn't matter
if your child drifts
to death
on white, feathered wings.

## Aborted Spring

I long to go back again.
My body is without shape
dragging its shadow along the corridor.
An invisible grayness
invades me.

I knock on every doorway
searching for her.
A door opens.
She stands there motionless,
lips pursed, eyes lifeless.
I beg her to let me in.
She doesn't.
The door closes.

I disintegrate.
My shadow leaves
six pomegranate seeds on her threshold.

## Bethlehem, 1984

The taxi speeds toward Bethlehem
hugging the khaki-colored rocks.
Sun-dried, wind-dried, unshorn sheep
huddle under Bedouin tents.
The earth is parched.
Only the blood-red pomegranate
and silver-leafed olive trees,
gnarled, cry survival in their ancient groves.
The desert breath drifts over
the golden dome of the Basilica.
In the courtyard
a wrinkled peddler unfolds accordion-pleated cards,
vendors display plastic creches,
Arabic songs blare from transistors
mingling with the muezzin's call.
Gears grinding, buses disgorge tourists
into the grotto.
Nikons flashing,
They seek the Holy Spot.

## The Chambered Nautilus

I often put my foot in my mouth,
but what the hell, that's the way I move.

Want to know where I come from?

Ask Aristotle.
Gave me my Greek name, *cephalopod*.

Aztecs carved me into the temple of Quetzalcoatl.
Warriors forced raucous notes from my throat.
Bellini crafted me into a jeweled goblet
only to be peddled at auction.

But it's useless.
You still can't fathom me.

I live deep within my hard shell
guarded by luminescence.
I keep on the move
trying to create the perfect chamber.

## Allium Cepa

What do you want to know about
this Asiatic herb
with its pungent edible bulb.

Its lineage ancient.
Egyptians accorded it divine powers,
inscribed it on their monuments.

I am not indifferent to its properties.
I peel off its layers, limpid, translucent.
I taste its liquid fire.

My mother takes them in her hands
before removing their outer skin.
She grasps her knife, cutting the onions
into fragile circles.
She places them in sizzling oil.

The odors envelop her,
burning her eyes.
Stirring rapidly, she subdues
the vapors with her wooden spoon
and never hears me leave, chanting
*Allium Cepa.*
*Allium Cepa.*

## To Mushrooms on Nantucket

Hidden under dark leaves,
you erupt magically
from your primeval breeding place.

You invoke remembrances,
elves, toadstools,
Indian pipes in pine forests.

I touch your fragile caps.
Your spores contaminate me,
each a possible killer.

Sorcerer, how will I know you?

**Emily, can we talk?**

Enough of your dashes and capitals and tight-assed four liners.
You're everywhere these days.
Your monastic face stamped
on shopping bags from Barnes & Noble.
Lots of mileage—

So let's talk,
just the two of us.
Tell me who's really
in that white dress.
C'mon, Emily.
Give me a break.

## Dining in the Hamptons

I stand at the window
watch the greedy rays of sun
slip past you
darting round the room
like photons rushing to illuminate
a television screen.

Sipping Margaux, I tell you
I was walking down Madison Avenue
and saw this man, hunched over,
asking for something, anything.

You do not hear me,
but then again, do I hear myself?
You stand by me,
watch the sun cauterize my words.

## The Drowned City

Mask in place, I sink
into the turquoise of my Aegean Sea.
Weightless, I drift downward,
downward
to my drowned city.

I'm phosphorescence
illuminating the disconnected walls,
reaching out for
the shattered amphorae.
I'm a shark

thrusting my way
through silt-covered streets,
ripping out encrusted barnacles.
I gather my broken shards,
tearing off my mask.

## Blue Leaves

"Would you tell me please," said Alice, a little timidly,
"why you are painting those roses?"
*Alice in Wonderland*

It took me a long time
to see that leaves weren't blue.

I picked up my crayon,
outlining each leaf, each stem, each vein.

Over and over again,
the blue seeping into my fingers.

In the classroom, she stood over me
blocking out all color.

I was afraid she would scream,
"Off with her head! Off with her head!"

## Hopper's Paintbrush

I never liked those long empty streets.

Shadows stretched out
along the acid green sidewalk.

Narrow windows
laid out like coffins.

Red and white barber's pole
tilted like an armless wooden soldier.

And that final painting,
you and Jo, up on the stage.

Two pantomime figures
holding hands, bowing.

Get back here, Hopper.
Help me drag in the junk.

The hunks of plywood,
the milk crates,
the plastic tarpaulin,
the stained couch,
the guy sleeping in the doorway,
the huddled figures on the heat grate.

Mix your paint with the stench of their bodies.
Then slap it on the canvas.

## The Walkman, 1984

I don't have time to slow down.
Years, like marathon runners,
try to outdistance me.

Daily,

I grab my t-shirt, sneakers, tights, leotard,
sweatband, lap counter, pulse meter,

harness Walkman,

slip on headphones.

And he sets the pace.

**Hey Google**

Hey Google, come down out of that cloud.
Who do you think you are?
Zeus!

Yeah, I know you're the great search engine.
What's quinoa? My African violet won't bloom! Best vacuums!
and on and on and on....

But take stock, Google.
We may need you,
but you need us, too.

## It Is a Hunger

It is a hunger.
I turn my head back to listen.

A man hacks the undergrowth
searching for the sacred wood.
Squats on his haunches, carving
an essence. His instruments govern him.

Slowly, the shape appears.
Sinewy neck joins head to body.
Heavy-lidded eyes stare out.
Arms embrace the hollowed-out abdomen.
Objects buried within the womb-like crypt.

I enter it
circling the mother and child,
touching jagged rocks,
crouching on the cone.

I feel nothing.

## My Mother the Candymaker

Martha 1925

She sure learned fast
for a newcomer to these shores.
Whizzed through Ellis Island

into bobbed hair, plucked brows,
cupid lips, line drawn to perfection,
feet tapping, "Ain't she sweet,

see her comin' down the street,"
luscious as the chocolate candies
she melts and molds and fills

with nuts and fruits and caramel,
each one, hand dipped, and hardly
notices me waiting for a lick.

## Laundromat

Where is this place?
Machines lined up
waiting for instructions.

Activate them with coins,
separate colors,
separate delicates.
Throw in that powder with its
        enzymes
                stabilizers
                        buffering agents.
Watch out for that tattletale gray,
that ring around the collar.

Don't over bleach.
Don't overload.
Don't overstay.

## The Photograph on My Mother's Bureau

Mother and child
laminated in time
on the oval metal frame.

The woman wears
a black velvet dress,
a silk scarf draped loosely
around her shoulders,
her short hair marcelled.

Looking down
at the child in her arms,
the lens freezes
her smile.

Arms outstretched
the child reaches
toward the unseen.

## Propolis

Through the city of cells,
the bee thrusts her body
scrutinizing the narrow streets
with her multifaceted eyes,

seeking the sacred resin
that will stop
the cold winds of winter
from entering her hive.

With jagged jaws,
she rips resin from the tree bark,
stuffs it into her pollen sacs, and moves slowly
home through honey corridors.

But I,
when the cold winds of winter
pierce my honeycomb,
where shall I find the sacred resin
to close the crevices of my hive?

## Reliquary

Dad gave it to me when I was nine,
this leather box
painted with violets that curl
out of heart-shaped leaves.
The calf skin, cracked and brittle,
now hangs in shreds.
The clasp broken
from the many openings.
You barely see my name scrawled
across the top.

Inside, a lonely silver elf shoe
no bigger than my thumbnail
on a patch of velvet.

A Christmas card I drew
of a house I never lived in.

A Cracker Jack pinkie ring,
an unfinished cross-stitched sampler,
stamps, cut-outs, marbles, and coins.
All still in my closet.

## The Rocking Chair in the Attic

*Daughter*
You got me, old rockin' chair,
all the years of my life lulling me,
cradling me on your curved pieces of wood.
Back and forth, to and fro,
hypnotic,
ticking off time.
You played me like an instrument.
Rock-a-bye-baby, don't you see.
You haven't gone anywhere.

*Mother*
I hid it in the attic,
stripped it of its motion,
made it powerless.
Yet still she looks for it
longing to clamber back
into Aunt May's waiting arms.
Long dead,
fat May sits there.
Waiting,
and like a bitch in heat,
she laps my child.
Rock-a-bye-baby, it's time to get off.

## Arachne

Envious, you seized me,
struck me with your spindle.

Desperate, I wrapped a rope
around my neck.

You cut me down,
changed me into a spider.

Now you, Athena,
are entombed in museums,
while I, Arachne, am alive,
spinning my web, world wide.

### Switched-on Brush

I will teach you, my Sensei,
how to use a computer.
Pack away your four treasures,
brush, ink stone, ink stick, and paper.

Flick on the switch,
Sensei, you are in command.
Drag the mouse to the menu bar
And create new files, Sensei.

Forget your traditions.
Try new fonts: Yellow Tail, Alegreya,
Alternate Gothic, Tisa.

Want bold? Just click.
Italics? Done!
Know how long that takes
with a bamboo brush?

C'mon, Sensei, what's it going to be,
Mac or PC?

## Variations on an Ode of Horace

Down dashes the wind!
Down with the speed of a dart,
crushing the thick-ribbed ice,
killing the quavering hart.

Shivering trees cringe low,
ashen-white with fear;
Chattering brooks now stammer,
feeling their end is near.

Outside, clear-blue coldness.
Inside, dim-red warmth.

Come fire, come wine, come song.
Burn from my brooding mind
worries and fears for others.
Trouble enough I'll find.

## Unbound

Crippled, that's how you wanted me.
I was rising from the navel of the earth
crashing through wild rocks
into the blinding white sun.

I was singing out,
fluent as the radiant Euterpe
winding lavender and myrtle in my hair.
Soaring.

You caught me in flight,
lured me earthward.
then bound my feet.
Blood and flesh mashed into pulp.

You wrapped each foot over and under
with strips of silk.
You shoved the stumps
into black velvet slippers.

I watched you.

At night I called out to the Muses,
Euterpe and her sisters.
All nine shimmering, came to my side.

They ripped off my slippers,
I limped away on my own feet.

**Marie Georges Fochios** was born in Pennsylvania in 1925 and moved to New York City with her Greek immigrant family during the Depression of 1929. With the advantage of free tuition, Marie graduated from Hunter College in 1946. Her love of learning continued to thrive for many semesters of graduate studies at Columbia University while she raised a family and worked as a fourth grade teacher at PS 24 in the Bronx for many decades. Her natural athleticism would erupt at certain times of her life in the form of being a member of her college fencing team, scuba diving in the Mediterranean with archeologists searching for Odysseus's ships, sailing to Bermuda with her husband, running the New York City Marathon at the age of 70, and engaging in a few triathlons with family and friends. Engaged with and inspired by English Romantic poets, (Keats, Shelley, and Byron, among others), she would write poems for her own pleasure over the years. Recently, at the urging of mentors, she published a poem in *Passagers*, resurrected some of her older works, wrote and revised more recent works, and is now presenting her first collection of reflections from her long and fruitful life.

www.ingramcontent.com/pod-product-compliance
Lightning Source LLC
Chambersburg PA
CBHW022052080426
42734CB00009B/1312